THE YEAR YOU WERE BORN
1970

A fascinating book about the year 1970 with information on events of the year, births, sporting events, the cost of living, movies, music, world events and adverts throughout the book.

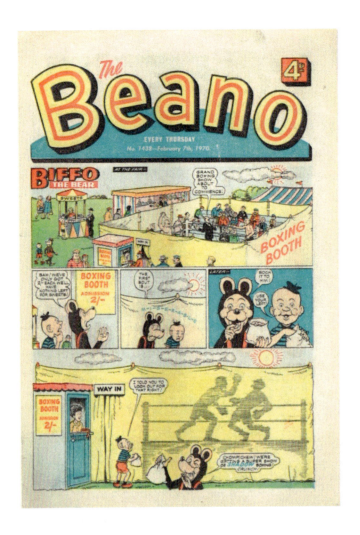

INDEX

Page 3   **Fashion**
Page 5   **Events of the year UK**
Page 13 **Adverts in 1970**
Page 18 **Cost of living**
Page 21 **Births**
Page 27 **Sporting events**
Page 31 **Movies**
Page 38 **Music**
Page 46 **World Events**
Page 57 **People in power**

FASHION 1970

It's an understatement to say that the 70s fashion styles were a bit far out. But for those of us who wore them, they were the ultimate in groovy fashion! Wild prints, shoes that added 5 inches to your height, polyester suits, short shorts that left little to the imagination, and skirts in three distinctly different lengths were just part of the 70s fashion fare. Indeed, the 70s had it all!

Though some 70s fashion trends carried over from the 1960s, including bell bottom trousers and tie-dyed shirts, many new styles were distinctly 70s.

And those of us who grew up during the era took our cues from those we saw on both the little screen and the big screen. Every teen wanted a mini dress like Marcia Brady's and young men admired John Travolta's gleaming white three-piece Saturday Night Fever suit. Nothing was too gaudy for the 70s!

70s Skirt

While the mini skirt of the 1960s was still ultra-popular in the following decade, women who didn't want to sport their legs now had more choices that still allowed them to look fashionable.

Dresses and skirts now came in three lengths – the traditional mini, the new midi – which landed between the knee and the ankle, and the maxi, which reached to the floor.

Coats came in the same lengths so that women could coordinate their outfits. Maxi skirts and long "granny" dresses were especially popular for formal events.

The granny dresses were often paired with chokers bearing cameos for the Victorian look that became quite popular during the 70s.

70s Trousers

For both men and women, bell bottoms were still easy to find on the racks of the most popular stores.

However, the ladies also sported "hip huggers", jeans that sat several inches below the normal waistline. These jeans or "dungarees" were often astoundingly tight and their owners were eager to decorate them with embroidery or studs and may have even bleached them to vary the color.

Men, similarly, weren't averse to wearing tight jeans and trousers, too. Velvet or lame trousers weren't unusual either.

Later in the decade, leisure suits – fashioned from a variety of colours of polyester fabric ranging from baby blue and mint green to brown – were all the rage and were a trend most agree need not ever be repeated.

Also in the late 1970s, both men and women squeezed into jumpsuits, one-piece outfits that zipped up the front and were usually worn with a wide belt. It was also a questionable trend, especially for those who were less than slim!

70s Shirts

Whereas men's dress shirts of the 60s generally included small, button-down collars, men of the 70s wore shirts in solids and loud prints with long, pointed collars. The print shirts were often paired with the aforementioned leisure suits.

Ladies shirts ran the gamut from peasant-style, flowy tops that had become popular in the late 1960s to skimpy halter tops that were pared with equally-skimpy shorts known as hot pants. Sequined bra tops were also a common trend and, later, tube tops – a strapless sleeve of stretchy fabric that pulled over the head and covered the upper torso – were all the rage.

70s Accessories

In the 70s, traditional belts were often replaced by beads or handmade macramé creations. Large peace sign necklace or surfer's crosses were worn around the neck on heavy chains, attesting to the importance of peace to those who were growing up during this era following the Vietnam Conflict.

But the most notable accessory of the 70s had to be the platform shoe. Worn by women of all ages and some men as well, these shoes were in every hip store in the country and some not-so-hip shops as well. The soles on these shoes, boots, or sandals ranged from about 2 to 4 inches thick. Many of them were fashioned in wild prints, some were glittery, and others were even transparent.

They may have made it difficult to walk, but every self-respecting 70s girl and hip guy had at least a few pairs in their closet. Later in the decade, the antithesis of this flamboyant shoe was introduced. In contrast, the "Earth Shoe", a product of Scandinavia, sported a thick sole and a thin heel, the opposite of most traditional shoes.

The Earth Shoe was very plain. Made of leather, it usually tied or included a large front buckle and was touted by nature lovers as the perfect shoe for hiking and enjoying other outdoor pursuits.

70s Hairstyles Women, 70s Hairstyles Men

The 1970s has become known for a lot of outlandish trends, and the hairstyles of that era are no exception.

As those who lived through the decade thumb through pictures of the decade's unique looks, they often snicker at the unusual hairstyles they sported, determined not to repeat the same mistake again!

But those unique hairdos were pretty cool in their day and those who wore them were quite proud of their look. And even though the young generation of today might find those styles unappealing, the looks of the 70s will remain some of the most memorable hairstyles in history.

EVENTS OF THE YEAR

The half Crown was taken out of circulation on the 1st January 1970 a year before decimalisation. The coin had been in circulation since 1549 in the reign of Edward VI. The half crown was equivalent to two shillings and a sixpence.

January

1st   The National Westminster Bank began trading following merger of National Provincial Bank and Westminster Bank

Control of London Transport passed from the London Transport Board to the London Transport Executive of the Greater London Council, except for country area (green) buses which passed to London Country Bus Services, a subsidiary of the National Bus Company.

18th   The grave of Karl Marx was vandalised by anti-Germanic racists at Highgate in London.

22nd   The first jumbo jet carrying fare-paying passengers has arrived at Heathrow airport. The newly-constructed Boeing 747, Pan Am Flight Two, touched down at Heathrow at 1414GMT today - seven hours late due to technical problems. The jumbo had brought 324 passengers across the Atlantic from New York to London.

February

3rd The Avenger was significant as it was the first and last car to be developed by Rootes after the Chrysler takeover in 1967. Stylistically, the Avenger was undoubtedly very much in tune with its time; the American-influenced "Coke Bottle" waistline and semi-fastback rear-end being a contemporary styling cue, indeed the Avenger would be the first British car to be manufactured with a one piece plastic front grille. It was similar in appearance to the larger Ford Cortina Mark III (1970–1976), which was launched later in 1970.

However, from an engineering perspective it was rather conventional, using a 4-cylinder all-iron overhead valve engine in 1250 or 1500 capacities driving a coil spring suspended live axle at the rear wheels. The Avenger was immediately highly praised by the press for its good handling characteristics and generally good overall competence on the road and it was considered a significantly better car to drive than contemporaries like the Morris Marina.

13th Black Sabbath released their **self titled debut album** in the UK, credited as the first major album in the **heavy metal**.

19th Prince Charles, the Prince of Wales joins the Royal Navy.

23rd Rolls Royce ask the government for £50,000,000 to help towards the development of the RB 211-50 Airbus jet engine.

March

6th The importation of pets was banned after an outbreak of **rabies** in **Newmarket, Suffolk**.

12th **Quarantine** period for cats and dogs was increased to one year as part of the government's anti-**rabies** measures.

17th **Martin Peters**, who scored for England in their 1966 World Cup final win, became the nation's first £200,000 footballer in his transfer from **West Ham United** to **Tottenham Hotspur**.

23rd Eighteen victims of **thalidomide** were awarded a total of nearly £370,000 in compensation.

April

1st Everton won the Football League First Division title.

10th The Elton John album is released, the second album by Elton John, but the first to be released in the United States.

11th Chelsea and Leeds United drew 2–2 in the FA Cup final at Wembley Stadium, forcing a replay.

18th British Leyland announces that the Morris Minor, its longest-running model which had been in production since 1948, would be discontinued at the start of next year and be replaced with a new larger car available as a four-door saloon and three-door fastback coupe, and possibly a five-door estate by 1975.

28th David Webb scored the winning goal (pictured below) as Chelsea defeated Leeds United 2-1 in the FA Cup final replay at Old Trafford, gaining them the trophy for the very first time

May

19th The government made a £20,000,000 loan available to help save the financially troubled luxury car and aircraft engine manufacturer Rolls Royce.

22nd A tour by the South African cricket team was called off after several African and Asian countries threaten to boycott the Commonwealth Games.

24th The Britannia Bridge, carrying the railway across the Menai Strait, was badly damaged by fire.

28th Bobby Moore, captain of the England national football team, was arrested and released on bail in Bogotá, Colombia, on suspicion of stealing a bracelet in the Bogotá Bracelet incident.

29th Law Reform (Miscellaneous Provisions) Act abolished actions for breach of promise and the right of a husband to claim damages for adultery with his wife

June

1st Prime Minister **Harold Wilson** is hit in the face with an egg thrown by Richard Ware, a **Young Conservative** demonstrator.

2nd **Cleddau Bridge**, in **Pembrokeshire**, collapsed during erection, killing four, leading to introduction of new standards for **box girder bridges.**

10th Just a few months after the Conservatives had enjoyed opinion poll leads of more than 20 points, opinion polls were showing Labour several points ahead of the Conservatives with eight days to go before the general election. If Labour won the election, it would be a record third consecutive general election win for the party and would probably result in the end of **Edward Heath**'s five-year reign as Conservative leader.

14th England's defence of the **FIFA World Cup** ended when they lost 3–2 to **West Germany** at the quarter final in **Mexico**.

17th **British Leyland** created a niche in the **four-wheel drive** market by launching its luxury **Range Rover**, which was to be marketed as a more upmarket and urban alternative to the utilarian **Land Rover** that had been in production since 1948.

19th The general election results are announced and Edward Heath's Conservative Party wins with a majority of 30 seats, a major surprise as most of the opinion polls had shown that **Harold Wilson**'s Labour were likely to stay in power. Among the new Members of Parliament are: future party leaders **Neil Kinnock** and **John Smith** for Labour, and **Kenneth Clarke** and **Geoffrey Howe** for the Conservatives.

21st British golfer **Tony Jacklin** wins the **U.S. Open**.

29th Caroline Thorpe, 32-year-old wife of **Liberal Party** leader **Jeremy Thorpe** and the mother of his two-year-old son Rupert, dies in a car crash.

July

3rd Three civilians were killed and 10 troops injured when British Army soldiers battled with IRA troops in Belfast.

Dan-Air Flight 1903: 112 were killed when a **Manchester** to **Barcelona** flight crashed in the mountains of Northern Spain, there were no survivors.

14th 5 speedway riders die in Lokeren, Belgium when a minibus carrying members of the West Ham speedway team crashed into a petrol tanker after a brief tour. One of those killed was Phil Bishop, a founding member of the West Ham speedway team from before WW2.

15th Dockers voted to strike leading to the **docks strike of 1970**. Dockers struck for a pay rise of £11 per week on 15 July 1970 and around 47,000 dockers were involved nationally.

16th The 1970 British Commonwealth Games were held in **Edinburgh, Scotland**, from 16 July to 25 July. This was the first time the name **British Commonwealth Games** was adopted, the first time **metric units** rather than **imperial units** were used in all events, and also the first time the games were held in **Scotland**. Also, these games saw the first unique Games trademark logo: an emblem showing the Games emblem intertwined with a St Andrews Cross and a thistle. They were followed by the **1970 Commonwealth Paraplegic Games** for wheelchair athletes.

31st The last issue of **grog** in the **Royal Navy** was distributed. Grog is any of a variety of **alcoholic beverages**. The word originally referred to a drink made with **water** and **rum**, which British **Vice Admiral Edward Vernon** introduced into the naval squadron he commanded in the West Indies on 21 August 1740. Vernon wore a coat of **grogram** cloth and was nicknamed Old Grogram or Old Grog. The **Merriam–Webster Collegiate Dictionary**, which agrees with this story of the word's origin, states that the word "grog" was first used in this sense in 1770. Following **England's conquest of Jamaica** in 1655, a half-**pint** of **rum** gradually replaced beer and **brandy** as the drink of choice. Given to the sailor straight, this caused additional problems, as some sailors saved the **rum rations** for several days to drink all at once. Due to the subsequent illness and disciplinary problems, the rum was mixed with water.

August

9th Police battle with black rioters at Notting Hill, London

20th England national football team captain Bobby Moore was cleared of stealing a bracelet while on World Cup duty in Colombia.

26th The third Isle of Wight Festival attracted over 500,000 pop music fans, with appearances by Jimi Hendrix, The Who, The Doors and Joan Baez. The festival lasted for six days.

27th The Royal Shakespeare Company's revolutionary production of Shakespeare's A Midsummer Night's Dream, directed by Peter Brook, opened at Stratford.

September

9th BOAC Flight 775 was hijacked by the Popular Front for the Liberation of Palestine after taking off from Bahrain—the first time a British plane had been hijacked.

18th American rock star Jimi Hendrix, 27, died in London from a suspected drug-induced heart attack.

19th The first festival at Worthy Farm was the Pilton Pop, Blues & Folk Festival, mounted by Michael Eavis (pictured below) on Saturday 19 September 1970, and attended by 1,500 people. The original headline acts were The Kinks and Wayne Fontana and the Mindbenders but these acts were replaced at short notice by Tyrannosaurus Rex, later known as T. Rex. Tickets were £1. Other billed acts of note were Quintessence, Stackridge, and Al Stewart.

The first Glastonbury Festival at Pilton Farm

October

3rd Tony Densham, driving the "Commuter" dragster, set a British land speed record at Elvington, Yorkshire, averaging 207.6 mph over the flying kilometre course

5th BBC Radio 4 first broadcast consumer affairs magazine programme You and Yours; it would still be running nearly 50 years later.

12th After a debacled launch only eighteen months previously, British Leyland announce a much improved Austin Maxi featuring a new gear change, increased engine size and much improved trim, answering many of the critical points raised by the motoring press at the car's original launch.

15th The last narrow boats to carry long-distance freight commercially on the canals of the United Kingdom arrived with their last load, coal from Atherstone for a West London jam factory.

19th British Petroleum discovered a large oil field in the North Sea.

23rd The Mark III Ford Cortina went on sale. At launch a full range of models are offered including two-door and estate variants. Unlike previous models, this Cortina was developed as a Ford Europe model sharing the floor-pan with the similar German Ford Taunus

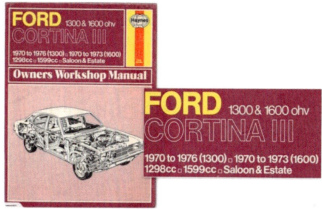

November

17th   The first page 3 model was placed in the Sun newspaper.

20th   The Ten shilling note ceased to be legal tender.

27th   The Gay Liberation Front organised its first march in London.

December

10th   Bernard Katz won the Nobel Prize in Physiology or Medicine jointly with Ulf von Euler and Julius Axelrod "for their discoveries concerning the humoral transmitters in the nerve terminals and the mechanism for their storage, release and inactivation"

26th   Athlete Lillian Board, 22, died in Munich, West Germany, after a three-month battle against cancer.

31st   Paul McCartney filed a lawsuit against the other members of The Beatles to dissolve their partnership, effectively ending the band.

ADVERTS IN 1970

Favourites for Christmas! FLEETWAY ANNUALS

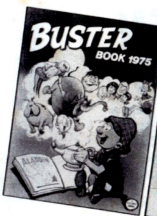

These all-time favourite annuals cater for children of all ages and tastes. Priced from 60p to £1.00 . . . they make ideal Christmas reading.

For children up to six years there's a choice of many happy annuals packed with colourful picture-stories. Look out especially for DISNEYLAND, JACK AND JILL BOOK, PLAYHOUR and TEDDY BEAR.

Boys and girls will enjoy the fun and laughter-packed BUSTER BOOK, WHIZZER AND CHIPS, COR!!, SHIVER AND SHAKE, KNOCKOUT. And boys who prefer sport and action stories will be delighted with SHOOT, VALIANT, TIGER, SCORCHER, and LION . . . Girls will thoroughly enjoy the picture-stories and features of TAMMY, PINK, JINTY, MUSIC STAR, PRINCESS TINA, PRINCESS TINA PONY BOOK, PRINCESS TINA BALLET BOOK No. 7 . . . and JUNE ANNUAL.

They're all great gifts

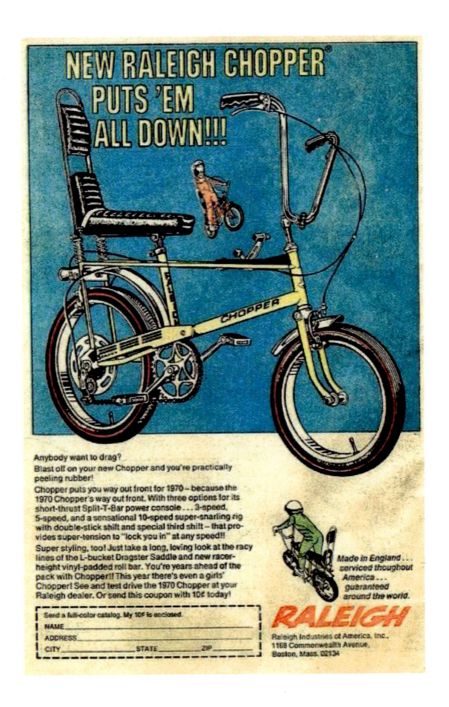

The Raleigh Chopper is a children's **bicycle**, a **wheelie bike**, manufactured and marketed in the 1970s by the **Raleigh Bicycle Company** of **Nottingham, England**. Its unique design became a **cultural icon** and is fondly remembered by many who grew up in that period. The design was influenced by **dragsters**, **"chopped" motorcycles**, beach buggies, and even chariots.

Woolworths Supermarkets (trading as Woolworths and colloquially known as "Woolies") is an Australian **supermarket/grocery store** chain owned by **Woolworths Limited**. Founded in 1924, Woolworths along with **Coles** forms a near-**duopoly** of Australian supermarkets accounting for about 80% of the Australian market

Fine Fare was the name of a chain of supermarkets in the United Kingdom. It was famous for its Yellow Pack budget **own-label** range, a forerunner to today's **own brand basic ranges.**

The company was acquired by **Associated British Foods** in 1963. ABF appointed **James Gulliver** to the post of chairman of Fine Fare in 1967; he continued to lead the business until 1972. Seven years after the takeover by Associated British Foods, the turnover had grown from £75 million to £200 million

THE COST OF LIVING IN 1970

Things looked a lot different in 1970 compared with today. The 70's were about to bring many changes, changes in music, culture and also how we worked and lived .Below is a list of the most common goods and wages.

These prices were before decimalization. Prices increased in 1971 after decimalization.

Wages, average weekly	**£32**
Average house price	£4500
Bacon, Back (lb)	**32p (0.72p kg)**
Beef, rump steak (lb)	57p (£1.25 kg)
Beer, Larger (pint)	**20p**
Bread, White sliced loaf	8p – 10p
Butter 250g	**10p – 15p**
Calculator, generic	£10
Camera, Polaroid	**£6.40**
Camp bed	£2.98
Car, Mini Cooper	**£480 - £550**
Car, Range Rover (launched 1970)	£1998
Carrots (lb)	**3p**
Channel No5 Perfum 50cl	£3.19
Cheese, Cheddar (lb)	**18p**
Cigarettes, 5s, Park Lane	5p
Cigarettes, 10s, Players No 6	**10.5p**
Cigarettes, 20s, Cadets	9.5p
Cigarettes, 20s, Consulates	**21.5p**
Cigarettes, 20s, Players No 6 King Size	29p
Coffee, Instant 100g	**22p**
Confectionary, Drumstick Lolly	1p
Confectionary, Mars Bar	**2p**
Crisp (bag)	2.5p
Digestive Biscuits (pkt)	**3p**
Eggs (Dozen)	18p
Flour (lb)	**4p**
Fruit, Apples (lb)	8p
Fruit, Bananas (Bunch)	**14p**
Fruit, Lemon (each)	2.5p
Gramophone, Portable	**£21**
Ham, Cooked and sliced (lb)	48p
Hamburger, Wimpy's	**10p**
Heater, convector 2kw	£5.85
Jelly sweets (portion)	**Less than a penny**

Lamb, Loin (lb)	25p
LP, Record Vinyl	**£2.40**
Meal, Breakfast	13p
Fish & Chips	**25p**
School Dinners	10p
Milk, Pasteurised (Pint)	**4.5p**
Onions (lb)	5p
Petrol, Gallon	**31p**
Potatoes (lb)	2p
Radio, Portable	**£4.92**
Rent, 1 – room basement flat	£2.50
Ring, Diamond engagement	**£13.56**
Sewing Machine, electric	£35.20
Sugar 2lb	**2p**
Ticket, movie "Love Story"	30p – 90p
Ticket, Wembley Cup Final	**£2**
Train, London to Manchester 1 way	£1.20
Tomatoes (lb)	**14p**
Typewriter, electric	£20.00
Washing Machine, Twin Tub	**£96.65**
Whisky 750ml (bottle)	£2.50
Wine 750ml (Bottle)	**£1.00**

These prices may seem amazing today but when all you have in your pocket a week is £32.00 it doesn't go far.

BIRTHS OF 1970

Naomi Elaine Campbell was born on the 22nd May 1948 and is a model actress and business woman. Naomi's first public appearance came at the age of seven in 1978 and was featured in the music video for Bob Marley "Is this love" and at the age of twelve she was tap-dancing in the video for Culture Club's "I'll tumble 4 ya. In 1986 and still a student at the Italia Conti Academy of Theatre Arts she was spotted by Beth Boldt, head of the Synchro Model Agency and her career soon took off. At the age of 16 she appeared on the cover of Elle.

Amelia Fiona "Minnie" Driver was born in Marylebone, London on the 31st January 1970. She is an actress and singer/songwriter. She made her TV debut in 1991 advertising Right Guard deodorant and in the same year she was performing as a Jazz vocalist and guitarist. She also appeared on British TV with small parts in Casualty, The House of Elliot, Lovejoy and Peak Practice. Her filming roles came as supporting actress in Golden Eye, Sleepers, Big night and Grosse Pointe Blank. In 1998 she starred in the film Governess and Hard Rain along side Christian Slater and Morgan Freeman. In 2001 she signed up with EMI and Rounder Records with the song "Everything I got in my pocket". Her first album reached No34 in the charts and she had written 10 of the 11 songs. Minnie released her second album "Seastories" in 2007 and went on to produce a third in 2014 called "Ask me to dance". Her latest role is in the movie thriller "The Spinning Man" 2018 alongside Pierce Brosnan and Guy Pierce.

Simon John Pegg was born in Brockworth, Gloucestershire on the 14th February 1970. After graduating from Bristol University he made small appearances in Asylum, Faith in the future, Big Train and Hippies he also appeared in the World War II drama "Band of Brothers". Simon has also played in a host of films which include Tube Tales, The Parole Officer, Shaun of the Dead, Land of the Dead, Mission: Impossible III, Hot Fuzz, Diary of the Dead, Star Trek, Burke and Hare, Paul and The Worlds End to name but a few. Simon Pegg is also a massive Star Trek fan and was fortunate to get the part as Scotty the engineer. He had the same roll in the next two Star Trek films called Star Trek Into Darkness and Star Trek Beyond. Simon married his long term girl friend Maureen McCann in Glasgow on the 23rd July 2005 and beside him was his best friend Nick Frost as his best man. Simon also suffered with depression and alcoholism and promptly went into rehab for his drinking. Now fully recovered and enjoying life and work again.

Warwick Ashley Davis was born in Epsom, Surrey on the 3rd February 1970. Warwick was born with Spondylopiphyseal dysplasia congentia which is a rear form of dwarfism. At the age of 11 his mother heard an advert on the radio asking for people under the height of 4feet or shorter to play a role in Star Wars Return of the Jedi and Warwick got the part. Warwick also got the role of Professor Filius Flitwick in the Harry Potter films. Warwick is also a TV presenter, writer, director, producer and a comedian. Warwick got married in 1991 and had 4 children, unfortunately 2 had passed away. In addition to his acting career Warwick in 1995 co-founded a talent agency for actors less than 5 foot from which most of the dwarf actors starred in Star Wars, Willow, Labyrinth and the Harry Potter series.
In 2016 Warwick started the TV quiz show Tenable and given another 2 series thereafter. In April 2010 Warwick published his autobiography Size Matters Not: The Extraordinary Life and Career of Warwick Davis.

Alan Shearer was born in Gosforth, Newcastle Upon Tyne on the 13th August 1970. Alan Shearer is a retired English footballer who was regarded as one of the world's best strikers. Recognized for his skills at a tender age of thirteen, Shearer went on to play for various clubs such as Southampton, Blackburn Rovers and Newcastle United in a career spanning two decades. He also represented England in the 1998 FIFA World Cup. Alan has scored around 49 of his 206 goals for Newcastle only by headshots, a feat which is rarely achieved by most footballers. He is associated with various charities and even during his days as a footballer, he took time out for charitable causes. He also raised money for this organisation through various football matches. Alan has also started his own charity organisation 'The Alan Shearer Foundation'. In his playing days he was considered to be one of the richest footballers around the globe and still holds this reputation, even after his retirement.

Tamzin Maria Outhwaite was born on the 5th November 1970 from Ilford, London. A British actress who has starred in several television and theatre productions. She is best recognized for appearing as Melanie Owen on BBC's 'EastEnders' and as Rhoda Bradley on the British drama series 'Vital Signs'. Besides these, she is famous for portraying the roles of Rebecca Mitchell in the drama 'Hotel Babylon', of Rose Chamberlain in the series 'The Fixer' and of DCI Sasha Miller in the crime show 'New Tricks'. On stage, the British artiste has acted in plays such as 'Boeing Boeing', 'Sweet Charity', 'How the Other Half Loves', 'Grease' and 'Oliver', to name a few. Outhwaite has also starred in a handful of television films including 'When I'm 64', 'Walk Away and I Stumble', 'Frances Tuesday', 'Fast Freddie, the Widow and Me' and 'Final Demand'. She is a onetime National Television Award winner and two times British Soap Award winner. Extremely talented, she is also a stunning lady with a bold sense of fashion!

Helen Victoria Baxendale was born in Pontefract, West Yorkshire on the 7th June 1970. An English actress who appears on stage, television and in films. She is best recognized for her roles as Rachel in the British comedy-drama 'Cold Feet' and as Emily in the American sitcom 'Friends'. Both the shows that she acted in became extremely popular and received high ratings. She also earned praise for working on other television shows including 'Cardiac Arrest', 'An Unsuitable Job for a Woman', 'Adrian Mole: The Cappuccino Years', 'Dirk Gently' and 'Kidnap and Ransom'. She is currently playing a main role in the British-Irish sitcom 'Cuckoo'. Helen initially earned recognition as a stage actress after working in the following plays, 'Soldiers', 'After Miss Julie', 'The Woman Before', the Marowitz 'Hamlet', and 'Swimming with Sharks'.

Sadiq Aman Khan was born in Tooting, London on the 8th October 1970. A British solicitor and politician who is serving as the current Mayor of London, in office since 2016. He previously served as the Member of Parliament (MP) for Tooting from 2005 to 2016. Born and raised in a British Pakistani family He was a solicitor for a considerable period, working on cases that involved human rights, and for three years. He joined politics sometime in the early 1990s and from 1994 to 2006, served as a Councillor for the London Borough of Wandsworth. Khan was later appointed as the Minister of State for Transport. Khan's political views and résumé had already made him a popular figure in British politics when he decided to contest in the 2016 London mayoral election. Khan was eventually elected to the mayoral office with 56.8% of the vote, becoming London's first ethnic minority mayor.

Alexander Armstrong was born in Rothbury, Northumberland on the 2nd March 1970 and is most celebrated for his comedy partnership with Ben Miller, but he has worked in various other fields with much success, perhaps most surprisingly as a musician – he won a choral scholarship to Trinity College, Cambridge, plays the piano and oboe, has fronted his own band, and has presented a weekend show on Classic FM. Alexander has also released 3 albums; A Year of song in 2015 which reached number 6 in the charts, Upon a different shore in 2016 which reach number 8 in the charts and In a winters light in 2017 which got to 24 in the charts. Additionally Armstrong has acted in a range of TV and radio roles, and is a familiar primetime TV face as host of Pointless.

Darren Gough was born in Barnsley, South Yorkshire on the 18th September 1970. Darren was a right arm fast medium bowler and right hand batsmen and use to captain the side of Yorkshire. He made his England debut in test cricket and one day internationals in 1994. He was the spearhead of England's bowling attack through much of the 1990s, he is England's second highest wicket-taker in one-day internationals with 234, and took 229 wickets in his 58 Test matches, making him England's ninth most successful wicket-taker. He retired from Test cricket in 2003 due to a knee injury having taken 229 wickets with a bowling average of 28.39. In 2005, Gough took part in the BBC television show strictly come dancing, partnered with British National champion Lilia Kopylova. Gough noted that this would keep him fit whilst allowing him to spend the winter with his family and, visibly at least, had the support of his England colleagues. He went on to win both the main series and the 2005 Christmas Special. Two years later he returned to win the 2007 Christmas Special. Following this he took part in the Strictly Come Dancing live tour during January and February 2008.

Dame Kelly Holmes was born in Tunbridge Wells, Kent on the 19th April 1970. Kelly Holmes is a former British middle-distance runner who retired from athletics after her stunning success at the 2004 Olympic Games in Athens. As a teenager Kelly won the English Schools 1500m title at the age of only 13. Despite this early success and that her hero was Sebastian Coe; she decided to join the army at 18 and temporarily turned away from athletics. In the army she became British Army Judo champion and took part in army athletics events. In 2004 Holmes finally managed to get to an Olympic Games injury free, having been able to train properly all season. She took Gold in both the 800m and 1500m. This achievement was one of the most successful Olympic performances by a British Woman. The double victory also made her the oldest woman to win Olympic Gold at either, let alone both, the 800m and 1500m events.

Gareth Southgate OBE was born in Watford, Hertfordshire on the 3rd September 1970. Gareth played for Aston Villa, Middlesbrough (as captain), and Crystal Palace. Reached an FA Cup and UEFA Cup final as a player, and made 57 appearances for the England national team, featuring in the 1998 FIFA World Cup and both the 1996 and 2000 European Championships. Had a brief stint as manager for Middlesbrough before becoming a pundit for ITV Sport. Gareth managed the England U21 team from 2013 – 2016 and now manages the England nation team. In his first tournament the 2018 World Cup in Russia took England to the semi-finals which led him to win the Sports Personality of the year coach award. Gareth was appointed an Officer of the Order of the British Empire.

Martin Johnson CBE was born in Solihul, West Midlands on the 9th March 1970. Martin made his rugby union debut in 1989 for Leicester Tigers and had his England call up in 1993. He was also a late call up for the British Lion tour to New Zealand in 93. In 1999 he was given the captains arm band for England which he led for 39 matches. He captained the England team in the 1999 World Cup and reached the quarter finals then won the grand slam in 2003 and went on to lift the Rugby World Cup in the same year. This was to be his last international game for England making it 84 in total. On the 1st July 2008 he became the manager of England and won the six nations in 2011. He left his managerial position in November 2011 after the quarter final defeat in the Rugby World Cup and has not managed in rubgy since. Martin was awarded the Officer of the Most Excellent Order of the British Empire (OBE) in 1997 for his victorious success in the Lions tour to South Africa.

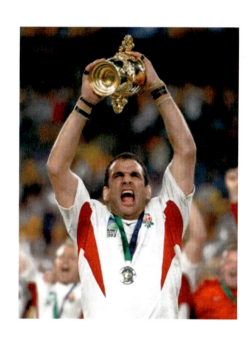

Melanie Sykes was born in Ashton-under- Lyne, Lancashire on the 7th August 1970. Melanie first came to television in the mid 1990's for a Boddingtons Bitter advert and also modelled for Berlie lingerie. Melanie's first job presenting was on The Big Breakfast. Melanie's TV career came to an abrupt holt until her break in hosting (along with Des O'Connor) Today with Des and Mel in 2003, but in May 2006 it was announced the show would be axed. Mel went on to present I'm A Celebrity Get Me Out of Here! and presented EastEnders Revealed and Gene Detectives on BBC1. Has hosted a number of award shows including Miss World, The BAFTAs and the Q awards. Has presented her own radio show on Galaxy FM.
Mel has her own line of underwear and lingerie with high street chain and retailer **Debenhams**. In June 2016, Sykes launched a lifestyle website which features fitness, food and lifestyle content as well as celebrity interviews and competitions.

SPORTING EVENTS

1970 British Grand Prix

The 1970 British Grand Prix was held at Brands Hatch on the 18th July 1970. The race was over 80 laps of the circuit. The total distance of the race was 212 miles. The race was won by pole sitter Jochen Rindt who beat Jack Brabham by 32 seconds in second place and Denny Hulme from New Zealand in third.

1970 FA Cup Final

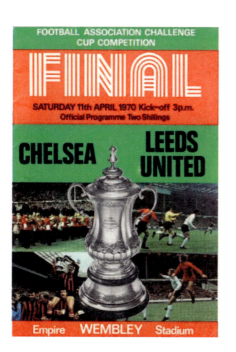

The **1970 FA Cup Final Replay** between Chelsea and Leeds United took place at Old Trafford, Manchester, after the first game was a 2-2 draw. It was the only time between 1923 and 2000 that a FA Cup Final was played at a stadium other than Wembley and the first FA Cup Final replay since 1912. The Chelsea line-up was unchanged from the first game, while the only change to the Leeds side was goalkeeper David Harvey replacing Gary Sparked. Chelsea would win the match 2-1 after extra time with a goal scored by David Webb in the 104th minute securing the club's first FA Cup title in their third appearance in a final. The game was watched on TV by over 28 million people which was a record for a FA Cup Final.

Football league division one champions 1969/70 season

During the **1969–70** English football season, Everton F.C. competed in the Football League First Division. They won their 7th League title finishing ahead of **Leeds United** and **Chelsea F.C.** Everton won 29 of the 42 games played drawing 8 games and only losing 5 games all season. They won the league with 66pts which does not seem a lot of points but in 1970 it was only two points for a win compared with 3 points today. The following season Everton could only finish in 14th position winning only 12 games.

County Cricket Champions 1970

The **1970 County Championship** was the 71st officially organised running of the **County Championship**. Kent won the Championship title.

County Championship table

Team	Pld	Won	Lost	Drawn	Batting bonus	Bowling bonus	Points
Kent	24	9	5	10	70	77	237
Glamorgan	24	9	6	9	48	82	220
Lancashire	24	6	2	16	78	78	216

In 1971 Kent finished fourth.

World Snooker Champion 1970

The 1970 World Snooker Championship was a snooker tournament that took place in 1970. Like the previous year the final was held at the Victoria Hall in London, from 6 to 11 April 1970. For the second and last time the event was sponsored by Player's No.6. Ray Reardon won in the final 37–33 against John Pulman. This year was the first of Reardon's six world titles; he held the title for only seven months until the next championship in Australia during November 1970. Reardon also made the highest break of the tournament with 118

Rugby Union Club Champions 1970

St. Helens won their sixth Championship when they beat Wigan 16-12 in the Championship Final. Wigan had ended the regular season as the league leaders. The Challenge Cup Winners were Leigh when they beat Leeds 24-7 in the final.

There was no county league competition this season; this was the first season in which the Lancashire League and Yorkshire League titles were no longer awarded. Leigh beat St. Helens 7–4 to win the Lancashire County Cup, and Leeds beat Featherstone Rovers 23–7 to win the Yorkshire County Cup.

1970 Grand National

The winner of the 1970 Grand National was a horse called Gay Trip ridden by Pat Taaffe and trained by Fred Rimell. Gay Trip was originally a flat racing horse and switched to national hunt racing when he was a five year old and won the Mackeson Gold Cup in 1969. For the 1970 National Pat Taaffe got the ride because Terry Biddlecombe was injured. Gay Trip was carrying top weight of 11 stone 5 pounds and had never run further than 2½ miles. Won by 20 lenghts.

The Open Championship 1970

Jack Nicklaus (The Golden Bear) won the Open at St Andrews on the old course in 1970. It was the 99th Open tournament played on the 8th – 12th July beating Doug Sanders in a Sunday play off. Jack had previously won the open in 1966.

Jack with his wife Barbara

Horse racing flat winners 1970

There really was only one horse to beat in 1970 and that was Nijinsky trained by Vincent O'Brien. The horse was unstoppable that year winning

Gladness Stakes
2000 Guineas
Epsom Derby
Irish Derby
King George VI and Queen Elizabeth Stakes
and The St. Ledger.

Nijinsky had raced 13 times winning 11 of them and his 2 defeats came at the end of a very long season at the Prix de l'Arc de Triomphe where he was second by a head to Sassafras. Less than 2 weeks after the Arc Nijinsky had his last race in the Champion Stakes where he was beaten by ¾ of a length by an English horse called Lorenzaccio and was put out to stud thereafter.

MOVIES 1970

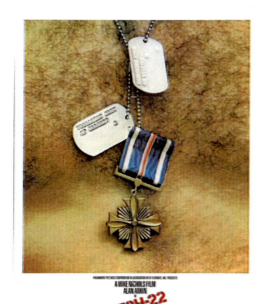

Catch 22. The story is about a bombardier in World War II tries desperately to escape the insanity of the war. However, sometimes insanity is the only sane way to cope with a crazy situation. Catch-22 is a parody of a "military mentality" and of a bureaucratic society in general. The director Mike Nichols wanted 36 B-25s to create the big army air force base but the budget could not stretch to more than seventeen flyable Mitchells. The Mexican location shooting took six months to complete because Cinematographer David Watkin would only film between 2pm and 3pm to make sure the lighting was the same.

The film cost around 18 million dollars to make and returned $24,911,670 at the box office.

The Aristocats. The story is about retired Madame Adelaide Bonfamille who enjoys the good life in her Paris villa with even classier cat Duchess and three kittens: pianist Berlioz, painter Toulouse and sanctimonious Marie. When loyal butler Edgar overhears her will leaves everything to the cats until their death, he drugs and kidnaps them. However retired army dogs make his sidecar capsize on the country. Crafty stray cat Thomas O'Malley takes them under his wing back to Paris. Edgar tries to cover his tracks and catch them at return, but more animals turn on him, from the cart horse Frou-Frou to the tame mouse Roquefort and O'Malley's jazz friends.

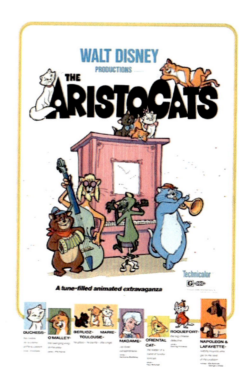

The film cost around $4,000,000 to produce and in the first weekend alone made $3,200,200. In total the film made $37,675,257 at the box office.

M·A·S·H. The personnel at the 4077 MASH unit deal with the horrors of the Korean War and the stresses faced in surgery by whatever means. The tone at the MASH is established by recent arrivals, surgeons Captains 'Hawkeye' Pierce, 'Duke' Forrest, and 'Trapper' John McIntyre - the latter who Hawkeye knows he's met somewhere, but Trapper who won't divulge where - whose antics can be best described as non-regulation, and in the negative words of one of their fellow MASH-ers: unmilitary. The unit's commanding officer, Colonel Henry Blake, doesn't care about this behaviour as long as it doesn't affect him, and as long as they do their job and do it well, which they do.

The film cost $3,500,000 to make and returned

$81,600.000 at the box office

Patton tells the tale of General **George S. Patton**, famous tank commander of World War II. The film begins with Patton's career in North Africa and progresses through the invasion of Europe and the fall of the Third Reich. Side plots also speak of Patton's numerous faults such his temper and tendency toward insubordination, faults that would prevent him from becoming the lead American general in the Normandy Invasion as well as to his being relieved as Occupation Commander of Germany.

Quote from Patton: Now I want you to remember that no bastard ever won a war by dying for his country. He won it by making the other poor dumb bastard die for his country.

The films budget was $12,000,000 and returned

$61,700,000 at the box office.

Love story of young adults Oliver Barrett IV and Jenny Cavilleri. Oliver comes from an extremely well off and old money New England family, the Barrett name which holds much gravitas and which is plastered especially all over Harvard where Oliver is in pre-law. Like those before him, he plans on attending Harvard Law School, which is not an issue in either the school not accepting him or he not wanting to attend. He has an extremely stiff relationship with his parents, especially his father, Oliver Barrett III, who loves his son in the old school way. Jenny, a music student at Radcliffe, comes from a working class Rhode Island background, she working her way through the program before she plans on going to Paris to further her studies. Unlike Oliver's relationship with his father, Jenny has a very casual one with her baker father, who she calls by his given name Phil.

The film cost $2,200,000 and returned $136,000,000 worldwide.

Kelly's Heroes. During World War II a German Colonel is captured by the Americans but before he can be interrogated an artillery barrage hits the camp. However, Ex-Lieutenant Kelly manages to reach the Colonel, get him drunk and learn that he is on a secret mission to ship $16,000,000 of gold to a base in France. Kelly is determined to get the gold and plans for himself and a few of his fellow soldiers to slip into enemy territory and steal the bullion.

The filming location was the coast south of Trieste, Yugoslavia.

The budget for the film was $4,000,000 and only returned $5,200,000.

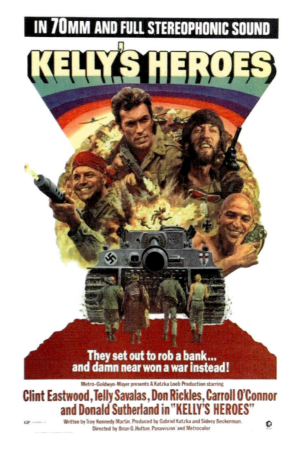

Two Mules For Sister Sara. Cynical Secession War veteran Hogan is in Mexico to earn a fortune trading arms to the Juarista rebels against the French troops of emperor Maximilian. He takes pity, with ever more mixed feelings, on maverick nun Sara, who is pursued by French cavalry. Godless Hogan never picks up she's ignorant in religious matters, while obviously the contrary in anything profane. Stuck on the wrong side of Mexican law and facing the semi-hostile Yaqui tribe, they mutually confide and find both to be heading for a French fort to be taken by the Juaristas, whose rustic 'colonel' Beltran only leads a bunch of war-ignorant peasants and requires him to fetch explosives from Texas. Only after they bond in several adventures, he learns her true crime and identity.

The budget was $2,500,000 and returned $5,050,000.

Airport. This precursor to later "epic" 70's disaster films illustrates 12 hours in the lives of the personnel and passengers at the "Lincoln Airport." Endless problems, professional and personal, are thrown at the various personnel responsible for the safe and proper administration of air traffic, airline management and aviation at a major US airport. Take one severe snowstorm, add multiple schedules gone awry, one elderly Trans Global Airlines stowaway, shortages, an aging, meretricious pilot, unreasonable, peevish spouses, manpower issues, fuel problems, frozen runways and equipment malfunctions and you get just a sample of the obstacles faced by weary, disgruntled personnel and passengers at the Lincoln Airport. Toss in one long-suffering pilot's wife, several stubborn men, office politics and romance and one passenger with a bomb and you have the film "Airport" from 1970.

Cost $10,000,000 to make and returned $100,489,150.

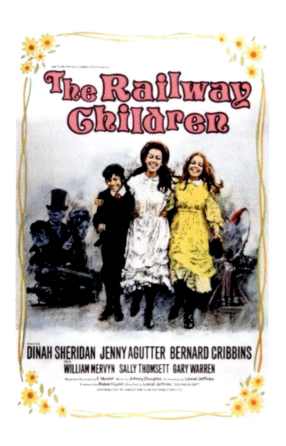

The Railway Children. The film opens in a happy, comfortable upper middle-class home in Edwardian London. One night in 1905, the three children see their father usher two strangers into his study. After an argument he leaves with them and does not return. They and their mother fall on hard times and eventually move to a cottage in the country.

Yet they keep their spirits up and find ways to help others. Fascinated by the nearby railway, they wave to the passengers faithfully every day, and their vigilance and courage prevent an accident.

Their kindness makes friends of some important people who can help solve the mystery of their missing father.

Lionel Jeffries read the book and loved it that much bought a six month filming right for £300.00.

Sally Thomsett was cast to play 11 year old Phyllis and she was actually 20 years old herself.

Beneath the Planet of the Apes. Brent is an American astronaut, part of a team sent to locate missing fellow American astronaut, George Taylor. Following Taylor's known flight trajectory, the search and rescue team crash lands on an unknown planet much like Earth in the year 3955, with Brent being the only survivor of the team.

What Brent initially does not know, much like Taylor didn't initially know when he landed here before Brent, is that he has landed back on Earth in the future, in the vicinity of what was New York City.
Brent finds evidence that Taylor has been on the planet. In Brent's search for Taylor, he finds that the planet is run by a barbaric race of English speaking apes, whose mission is in part to annihilate the human race. Brent eventually locates some of those humans, who communicate telepathically and who live underground to prevent detection by the apes.

The film cost $3,000,000 to produce and the box office returned $18,999,817.

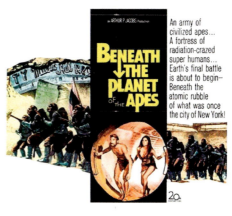

The Private life of Sherlock Holmes. Director Billy Wilder adds a new and intriguing twist to the personality of intrepid detective Sherlock Holmes. One thing hasn't changed however: Holmes' crime-solving talents. Holmes and Dr. Watson take on the case of a beautiful woman whose husband has vanished. The investigation proves strange indeed, involving six missing midgets, villainous monks, a Scottish castle, the Loch Ness monster, and covert naval experiments. Can the sleuths make sense of all this and solve the mystery?

Originally, the scenes featuring the Loch Ness Monster were intended to be filmed in the actual Loch. A life size prop was built which had several Nessie like humps which were used to disguise the flotation devices. The humps were removed, however, at Billy Wilder's request during a test run in the Loch the monster prop sank and was never recovered.

Chisum. As one of the founders of the town of Lincoln, John Chisum is increasingly worried as Lawrence Murphy moves in on the local stores, bank and land by questionable means. Chisum and fellow honest ranch owner Henry Tunstall try and use the law, but Murphy owns that too. Confrontation threatens and Tunstall's man Billy Bonney is not slow to get involved.

Men wore hats outside in Old West nearly 100% of the time. It was so rare that a man would remove his hat outside for more than brief periods that it would be the subject of discussion when or if it occurred. Multiple scenes in the film show men outside, hatless, and this is ignored or treated as "normal."

The film cost $4,000,000 to produce and the box office returned $6,000,000.

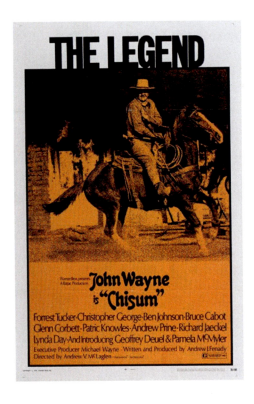

In the early 21st century, Dairylea Lunchables were advertised as being "full of good stuff", though the product contained high amounts of salt and saturated fats. Despite a 2007 reformulation that reduced salt content by 9% and saturated fat content by 34%, the claim "full of good stuff" was banned by the UK's **Advertising Standards Authority**

MUSIC 1970

The table below is a list of all the number one's in 1970, the name of the single and number of weeks at number one

Artist	Single	Week ending	Weeks at No1
Edison Lighthouse	Love Grows(where my rosemary goes)	31st January 1970	5
Lee Marvin	**Wand'rin Star**	**7th March 1970**	**3**
Simon & Garfunkel	Bridge Over Trouble Water	28th March 1970	3
Dana	**All kinds of Everything**	**18th April 1970**	**2**
Norman Greenbaum	Spirit in the sky	2nd May 1970	2
England World Cup Squad	**Back Home**	**16th May 1970**	**3**
Christie	Yellow River	6th June 1970	1
Mungo Jerry	**In the Summertime**	**13th June 1970**	**7**
Elvis Presley	The Wonder of You	1st August 1970	6
Smokey Robinson and The Miracles	**Tears of a Clown**	**12th September 1970**	**1**
Freda Payne	Band of Gold	19th September 1970	6
Mathews' Southern Comfort	**Woodstock**	**31st October 1970**	**3**
Jimi Hendrix Experience	Voodoo Child	21st November 1970	1
Dave Edmunds	**I Hear You Knocking**	**28th November 1970**	**6**

Edison Lighthouse

Love Grows (where my rosemary goes)

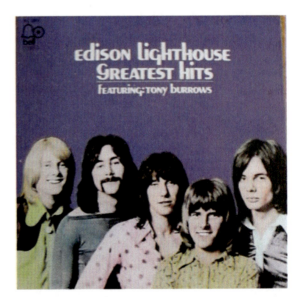

Edison Lighthouse was an English **pop** band, formed in **London**, England in 1969. The band was best known for their 1970 **hit single**, "Love Grows (Where My Rosemary Goes)" recorded in late 1969. The original line-up of Edison Lighthouse consisted of Tony Burrows (lead vocalist), Stuart Edwards (lead guitar), David Taylor (bass guitar), George Weyman (drums), and Ray Dorey (guitar). The group's Top 40 hit "Love Grows (Where My Rosemary Goes) was one of four near-concurrent UK Singles Chart Top Ten hit singles that Burrows released under different names."Love Grows (Where My Rosemary Goes)" was No. 1 for five weeks and sold 250,000 copies in the UK. It reached the top of the chart in its second week.

Lee Marvin

Wand'rin Star

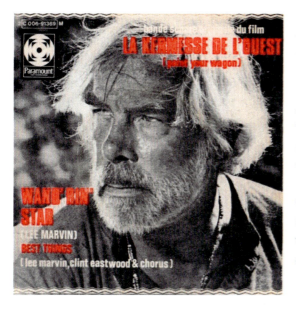

Aside from the Morricone Dollar single release, Wand'rin is arguably the most successful vinyl release among Eastwood related records. "Wand'rin Star" was a number one single in the UK and Ireland for Lee Marvin for 3 weeks in March 1970. Although rather strangely, the 7" UK release was one of the very few not to feature a full picture cover. A large amount of releases from around the world all seemed to benefit from a different cover apart from the generic Paramount sleeve that UK record buyers had to settle for. When the film of the musical was made in 1969, Lee Marvin took the role of prospector Ben Rumson. Not a natural singer, Lee Marvin sang all the songs in the film rejecting the idea to mime. Despite the film being a box office flop the soundtrack was a great success.

Simon & Garfunkel

Bridge Over Troubled Water

Bridge over Troubled Water was released on January 26, 1970, and several re-releases followed. The album was mixed and released in both stereo and quadraphonic. "Bridge over Troubled Water" is a song by American music duo **Simon & Garfunkel**. Produced by the duo and **Roy Halee**, the song was released as the follow-up single to "**The Boxer**" in January 1970. The song is featured on their fifth **studio album**, Bridge over Troubled Water (1970). Composed by singer-songwriter **Paul Simon**, the song is performed on piano and carries the influence of **gospel music**. The original studio recording employs elements of **Phil Spector**'s "**Wall of Sound**" technique using L.A. session musicians from the **Wrecking Crew**. Bridge Over Troubled Water made number 1 in the UK in March 1970 and stayed there for 3 weeks.

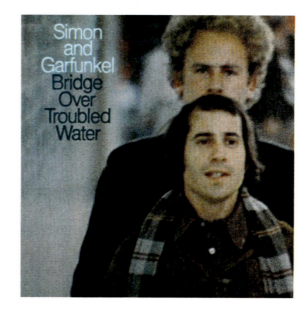

Dana

All Kinds of Everything

Dana had recorded "All Kinds of Everything" following her victory in the Irish National Song Contest with veteran Eurovision composer **Phil Coulter** ("**Puppet on a String**", "**Congratulations**") providing the musical arrangement for the Ray Horricks production. The record was released on 14 March 1970 on the **Rex** label for whom Dana had previously recorded four singles (including "Look Around") and became a massive hit in the Republic of Ireland even prior to its Eurovision win reaching number 1 on the chart dated 20 March 1970 and remaining at number 1 for nine weeks: in October 1970 Dana received a gold disc for "All Kinds of Everything" selling 100,000 units in Ireland. In the UK "All Kinds of Everything" was number 1 for the weeks dated 18 April and 25 April 1970.

Norman Greenbaum

Spirit in the Sky

"Spirit in the Sky" is a song written and originally recorded by **Norman Greenbaum** and released in late 1969. The single became a **gold record**, selling two million copies from 1969 to 1970. It became number one in the UK in April 1970 for two weeks. It also became number one in Australia and Canada and got to number 3 in America.

The song was featured on the 1969 album **of the same name**. Cover versions by **Doctor and the Medics** and **Gareth Gates** have also made the number 1 spot in the UK.

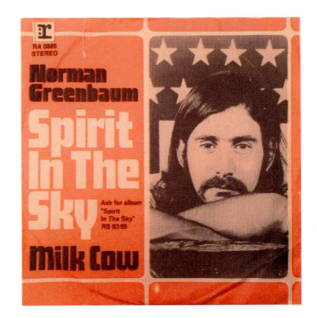

England World Cup Squad

Back Home

"Back Home" was a popular song written by Bill Martin and Phil Coulter. It was recorded by the 1970 England World Cup squad and released on the single Pye 7N 17920. It was produced by Martin and Coulter. The arrangements were made by Phil Coulter. The single, which began the tradition of the England squad recording World Cup songs to celebrate their involvement, reached number one on the UK singles chart for three weeks in May 1970. England were the reigning world champions at the time, having won the 1966 World Cup, but were knocked out in the Quarter Finals after a 3-2 defeat to West Germany. The B side of the 7" vinyl single was called "Cinnamon Stick", and was also sung by the England football team.

Christie

Yellow River

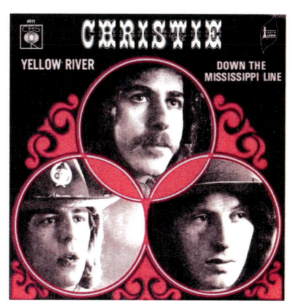

Yellow River is a popular song recorded by the British band **Christie** written by band leader Jeff Christie. Released on 23 April 1970, it became an international hit, reaching number one on the **UK Singles Chart** for one week in June 1970. In the US, it reached number 23 on the **Billboard Hot 100** singles chart. The actual location of Yellow River in this song is not specified, although the author, Jeff Christie, is on record as saying that it was inspired by the idea of a soldier going home at the end of the **American Civil War**. As the song was released during the **Vietnam War**, it has been interpreted as being about a soldier leaving the U.S. **Military** at the end of his period of **conscription**.

Mungo Jerry

In the Summertime

In the Summertime is the debut single by British rock band **Mungo Jerry**. Written and composed by its lead singer, **Ray Dorset**, it celebrates the carefree days of summer. In 1970, it reached number one in charts around the world, including seven weeks on the **UK Singles Chart**, two weeks on one of the **Canadian charts**, and number three on the **Billboard Hot 100** singles chart in the US. It became one of the **best-selling singles of all-time**, eventually selling 30 million copies.

Dorset has said that the song only took ten minutes to write, which he did using a second-hand **Fender Stratocaster** while he was taking time off work from his regular job, working in a lab for **Timex**.

Elvis Presley

The Wonder of You

Elvis Presley recorded a **live version** of "The Wonder of You" in **Las Vegas, Nevada** in February 1970. The song was released as a single on the 20th April, 1970, **backed by** the song "Mama Liked the Roses". In the United States, both songs charted at number 9 together in the spring of 1970.

"The Wonder of You" was one of his most successful records in the UK ever, topping the **UK Singles Chart** for six weeks in the summer of that year. It is his fifth biggest seller in the UK to date, with sales of 891,000. It also stayed at number one in the **Irish Charts** for three weeks that same year. This was the 59th **Top 40 hit** of his career.

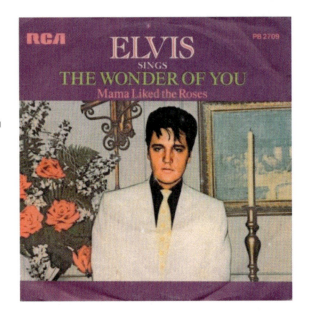

Smokey Robinson and The Miracles

Tears of a Clown

The Tears of a Clown is a song written by Hank Cosby, Smokey Robinson, and Stevie Wonder and originally recorded by Smokey Robinson & the Miracles for the Tamla Records label subsidiary of Motown. It was re-released in the United Kingdom as a single in July 1970, and it became a number 1 hit on the UK Singles Chart for the week ending 12 September 1970. Subsequently, Motown released "The Tears of a Clown" as a single in the United States as well, where it quickly became a number 1 hit on both the Billboard Hot 100 and R&B Singles charts. This song is an international multi-million seller and a 2002 Grammy Hall of Fame inductee. Its success led Miracles lead singer, songwriter, and producer Smokey Robinson, who had announced plans to leave the act, to stay until 1972.

Freda Payne

Band of Gold

The legendary song writing team of Holland–Dozier–Holland used the name Edythe Wayne because of a lawsuit in which they were embroiled with **Motown**. Ron Dunbar was a staff employee and producer for Invictus. When they first offered the song to Freda Payne, she balked at the idea of recording it, finding the material more appropriate for a teenager or very young woman while she was nearly 30 years old. Payne reluctantly gave in after much persuasion by Dunbar. Almost immediately following its release, the Payne record became an instant pop smash, reaching number three in the US and number one on the **UK singles chart** and remaining there for six weeks in September 1970, giving Payne her first gold record.

Mathews Southern comfort

Woodstock

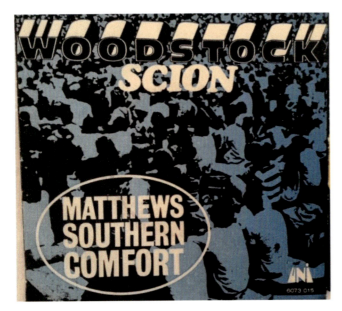

Iain Matthews (born Ian Matthews MacDonald, 16 June 1946) is an English musician and singer-songwriter. He was an original member of the British folk rock band **Fairport Convention** from 1967 to 1969 before leaving and forming his own band, Matthews Southern Comfort, which had a UK number one in 1970 with a cover version of **Joni Mitchell**'s song "**Woodstock**". The song was a number hit for 3 weeks. **Joni Mitchell** composed the song based on what she had heard from her then-boyfriend **Graham Nash** about the **Woodstock Music and Art Festival**. The lyrics tell a story about a spiritual journey to **Max Yasgur**'s farm, the place of the festival, and make prominent use of sacred imagery, comparing the festival site with the **Garden of Eden**

Jimi Hendrix Experience

Voodoo Child

Voodoo Child is a song recorded by the Jimi Hendrix Experience in 1968 that appears as the final track on the Electric Ladyland album released that year. After his death in 1970, Track Records released the song as a single in the United Kingdom using the title "Voodoo Chile. It became Hendrix's only number one single on the British record charts, reaching the top position during the week of November 15, 1970. It stayed at number one for one week. Several artists have performed or recorded versions of the song.

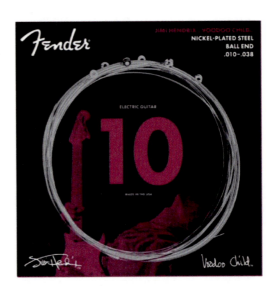

Dave Edmunds

I Hear You Knocking

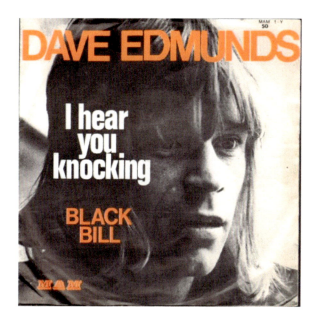

I Hear You Knocking is a rhythm and blues song written by Dave Bartholomew. New Orleans rhythm and blues singer Smiley Lewis first recorded the song in 1955. The lyrics tell of the return of a former lover who is rebuffed and Huey "Piano" Smith provided the prominent piano accompaniment in the style associated with Fats Domino.

"I Hear You Knocking" reached number two on the Billboard R&B singles chart in 1955, making it Lewis's most popular and best-known song. Subsequently, numerous artists have recorded it, including Welsh singer and guitarist Dave Edmunds, whose version reached number one in the UK for six weeks in 1970 and was in the top 10 in several other countries.

MUSIC ADVERTS 1970

WORLD EVENTS

January

5th On the 5th January 1970 a massive earthquake hit Tonghai County, Yunnan Province in China with a magnitude of 7.1 on the richter scale killing over 10,000 people. The earthquake cause about 25 million dollars worth of damage and was felt as far away as Hanoi, Vietnam 300 miles away.

14th Diana Ross and the Supremes preformed there last live concert together at the Frontier Hotel, Las Vegas. Diana Ross had here replacement Jean Terrell introduced at the end of the live performance to the adoring crowd.

20th It was announced that the Thames Barrier would be built. The barrier would stretch from Silvertown on the north bank to New Charlton on the south bank at a distance of 520 meters. The barrier was officially opened in 1984 by Queen Elizabeth II at a cost of £534 million.

21st Pan American Airways conducts its first commercial schedule flight from John F Kennedy airport to London Heathrow Airport.

26th Mick Jagger is fined £200 for the possession of cannabis.

31st The Jackson 5 has their first number one hit with "I want you back". It was their first TV appearance on the Diana Ross "The Hollywood Palace" show in October 1969 which got there recognition.

February

1st The Benavidez rail disaster happen killing 236 people and leaving 500 injured. Two trains collided after the train in front had a fuel injector fault and had to stop. After being stationary for over 40 minutes they failed to advise the train coming up the track of their problem and collided at 65mph completely crushing the rear carriage and shunting the local train 80 meters down the track.

10th An avalanche at Val-d'Isere in France kills 41 tourists.

11th Japan launch their first ever satellite into orbit called Ohsumi. Named after the province of Osumi in the southern islands of Japan.

13th Black Sabbath release their debut album called "Black Sabbath" and is considered to be the first Heavy Rock album.

19th The Poseidon Bubble finally burst. In the late 60's nickel was in high demand due to the Vietnam war but there was a shortage due to industrial action by the Canadian supplier Inco. Shares were initially sold at $0.80 per share and peaked at $280.00 per share then dramatically crashed.

21st Construction on the Bosphorus Bridge in Istanbul otherwise known as the 15 July Martyrs Bridge is the third bridge to connect Europe to Asia

22nd Guyana becomes a republic within the commonwealth of nations.

26th Chevrolet release their second generation of the Camaro. The car was heavily restyled and became much larger and wider.

March

1st Rhodesia severs all ties with the United Kingdom after announcing it has become a republic.

5th The Nuclear Non-Proliferation Treaty began with the agreement of 56 nations.

6th A group called the Weathermen constructed a bomb which was to be planted at a military dance in New Jersey accidently explodes killing the three terrorist.

7th Citroen introduce their new SM at the Geneva Auto Salon.

12th 18 – 20 year olds vote in a by-election in Bridgewater in the United Kingdom for the first time.

15th The Expo '70 world trade fair opens in Osaka, Japan

16th The New English Bible is completed

17th The U.S. Army charge 14 officers for withholding information relating to the My Lai Massacre. The massacre, which was later called "the most shocking episode of the Vietnam War", took place in two hamlets of Sơn Mỹ village in Quảng Ngãi Province. These hamlets were marked on the U.S. Army topographic maps as Mỹ Lai and Mỹ Khê. Between 350 and 500 unarmed people were killed.

18th United States Postal Service workers in New York City go on strike; the strike spreads to the state of California and the cities of Akro, Ohio, Philadelphia, Chicago, Boston, and Denver; 210,000 out of 750,000 U.S. postal employees walk out. President Nixon assigns military units to New York City post offices. The strike lasts two weeks

31st NASA's Explorer 1 satellite was launched on the 31st January 1958 and re-entered the earth's atmosphere on the 31st March 1970 after 12 years. It was the first spacecraft to detect the Van Allen radiation belt.

Japan Airlines Flight 351 was carrying 131 passengers and 7 crew from Tokyo to Fukuoka. It was hijacked by the Japanese Red Army. All passengers and crew were later released.

April

1st   The American president Richard Nixon signs the Public Health Cigarette Smoking Act banning all television adverts from the 1st January 1971.

The United States Census begins 1970. There are 203,392,031 residences on this day.

4th   Fragments of burnt human remains believed to be those of **Adolf Hitler, Eva Braun, Joseph Goebbels, Magda Goebbels** and the **Goebbels children** are crushed and scattered in the **Biederitz** river in **Magdeburg, East Germany**.

8th   A huge gas explosion at a subway construction site in Osaka, Japan kills 79 and injures over 400.

Israeli Air Force F-4 Phantom II fighter bombers kill 47 Egyptian school children at a school in what is known as Bahr el-Baqar massacre. The single-floor school was hit by five bombs and two air-to-ground missiles.

10th   Paul McCartney announces he has left the band The Beatles

11th   Apollo 13 is launched on its way to the moon. It was the seventh manned mission and the third to the moon. Apollo 13 returned to earth 6 days later despite all their problems.

16th   National Westminster Bank begins trading in the UK fir the first time.

17th   Apollo 13 Splashes down in the Pacific Ocean after 6 days.

22nd   The very first Earth Day is celebrated in the United States.

24th   China launches its first satellite called "Dong Fang Hong 1". It was launched using a Long March-1 Rocket.

26th   The World Intellectual Property Organization (WIPO) was found.

29th   The United States invade Cambodia in search of Viet-cong. Large antiwar protests break out over the United States.

May

1st President Richard Nixon orders U.S. forces to cross into neutral Cambodia, threatening to widen the Vietnam War, sparking protests across the United States and leading to the Kent State shootings.

4th Four students at **Kent State University** in **Ohio**, USA are killed and nine wounded by **Ohio National Guardsmen**, at a protest against the incursion into **Cambodia**.

6th **Charles Haughey** and **Neil Blaney** are dismissed as members of the **Irish Government**, for accusations of their involvement in a plot to import arms for use by the **Provisional IRA** in **Northern Ireland**.

8th The Beatles release their final album "Let it Be"

The New York Knicks win their first NBA championship, defeating the Los Angeles Lakers 113-99 in Game 7 of the world championship series at Madison Square Garden.

10th 100,000 people demonstrate against the Vietnam War in Washington D.C.

11th Lubbock tornado was a **tornado** event that occurred in **Lubbock, Texas**, on Monday, May 11, 1970. It was one of the worst tornadoes in **Texas** history, and occurred exactly 17 years to the day after the deadly **Waco Tornado**. It is also the most recent F5 **tornado** to have struck a **central business district** of a large city.

12th The 1976 Winter Olympics are awarded to **Denver, Colorado** but it was later withdrawn in 1972.

23rd A fire occurs in the **Britannia Bridge** over the **Menai Strait** near **Bangor**, Caernarfonshire, **Wales**, contributing to its partial destruction and amounting to approximately £1,000,000 worth of fire damage.

24th The **scientific drilling** of the **Kola Superdeep Borehole** begins in the **USSR**. The project is to drill as deep as possible into the earth's crust. The deepest the drill reached was recorded at 12,262 meters in to the earth.

31st The ninth FIFA World Cup was held in Mexico for the first time.

June

1st Soyuz 9, a two-man spacecraft, is launched in the **Soviet Union**. Soyuz 9 marks the longest manned flight by a solo spacecraft.

2nd Norway announces it has rich oil deposits of the north sea.

4th Tonga gains independence from the United Kingdom.

7th The Who becomes the first act to perform rock music (their **rock opera**, Tommy) at the **Metropolitan Opera House**, New York.

13th The Long and Winding Road becomes **the Beatles'** 20th and final single to reach number one on the US **Billboard Hot 100** chart.

18th The **Conservative Party** wins and **Edward Heath** becomes Prime Minister, ousting the **Labour** government of **Harold Wilson** after nearly six years in power. The election result is something of a surprise, as most of the opinion polls had predicted a third successive Labour win.

19th The **Patent Cooperation Treaty** is signed into **international law**, providing a unified procedure for filing **patent applications** to protect inventions.

21st Brazil beat Italy in the final of the World Cup 4 – 1 in Mexico

23rd The film Kelly's Heroes is released. (details under the movie section)

28th United States Army withdraw from Cambodia

30th **Riverfront Stadium** in **Cincinnati** opens. The Reds hosted Atlanta Braves in their first game. The stadium is now known as Cinergy Field. On the 29th December 2002 the stadium was demolished due to an implosion.

July

3rd The French Army detonates a 914 kiloton thermonuclear device in the **Mururoa Atoll**. It is their fourth and largest nuclear test.

4th A chartered Dan-Air De Havilland Comet crashes into the mountains north of Barcelona; at least 112 people are killed.

5th **Air Canada Flight 621** crashes at **Toronto International Airport**, Toronto, Ontario; all 109 passengers and crew are killed.

11th The first tunnel under the **Pyrenees** links the towns of **Aragnouet** (France) and **Bielsa** (Spain)

21st The High Dam, *as-Sad al-'Aali*, was completed. The Aswan high dam is 4,000 meters long and is 111 meters tall. The Dam contains 43,000,000 cubic meters of water.

23rd 2 CS gas canisters are thrown into the chamber of the British house of commons

30th Damages totalling £485,528 are awarded to 28 **Thalidomide** victims.

August

7th Harold Joseph Haley was a **Superior Court** judge in **Marin County, California**. He was taken hostage in his courtroom, along with several others, during the course of a trial, and was killed during the attempted escape of his captors with their hostages.

17th The United States sinks 418 containers of nerve gas into the Gulf Stream near the Bahamas.

18th Venera 7 is launched toward Venus. It later becomes the first spacecraft to successfully transmit data from the surface of another **planet.**

24th **Vietnam War** protesters **bomb** Sterling Hall at the **University of Wisconsin–Madison**, leading to an international manhunt for the perpetrators.

26th The Isle of Wight Festival 1970 begins on East Afton Farm off the coast of England. Some 600,000 people attend the largest rock festival of all time. Artists include Jimi Hendrix, The Who, The Doors, Chicago, Richie Havens, John Sebastian, Joan Baez, Ten Years After, Emerson, Lake & Palmer, The Moody Blues and Jethro Tull.

September

1st An assassination attempt against King **Hussein of Jordan** precipitates the **Black September** crisis.

5th Formula One driver Jochen Rindt is killed in qualifying for the Italian Grand Prix. He becomes World Driving Champion anyhow, first to earn the honour posthumously.

6th **Dawson's Field hijackings**, The **Popular Front for the Liberation of Palestine** hijacks four passenger aircraft from **Pan Am**, **TWA** and **Swissair** on flights to **New York** from **Brussels**, **Frankfurt** and **Zürich**.

9th Elvis Presley begins his first concert tour since 1958 in Phoenix, Arizona, at the Veterans Memorial Coliseum.

18th American musician **Jimi Hendrix dies at age 27** from an overdose of sleeping pills.

19th The first **Glastonbury Festival** is held, at a farm belonging to Michael Eavis.

20th Luna 16 lands on the Moon and lifts off the next day with samples. It lands on Earth September 24th 4 days later.

21st Monday Night Football debuts on ABC; the Cleveland Browns defeat the New York Jets 31–21 in front of more than 85,000 fans at Cleveland Stadium.

23rd The first women's only tennis tournament begins in Houston, known as the **Houston Women's Invitation**.

26th The Laguna Fire, previously known as the Kitchen Creek Fire and the Boulder Oaks Fire, occurred in 1970 in the **Laguna Mountains, San Diego, California**. In the end, the fire burned 175,425 acres and 382 homes, killing 16 people.

27th Richard Nixon begins a tour of Europe, visiting Italy, Yugoslavia, Spain, the United Kingdom and Ireland.

29th The U.S. congress gives permission for Richard Nixon to sell arms to Israel.

October

2nd Pink Floyd release their album Atom Heart Mother and becomes their first number one.

4th Janis Joplin Dies of a heroin overdose in her hotel room in Hollywood and was found by her producer Paul Rothchild.

5th The October Crisis occurred in October 1970 in the province of **Quebec** in **Canada**, mainly in the **Montreal metropolitan area**. Members of the **Front de libération du Québec (FLQ) kidnapped** the provincial Deputy Premier **Pierre Laporte** and British diplomat **James Cross**.

12th U.S. President **Richard Nixon** announces that the United States will withdraw 40,000 more troops from Vietnam before **Christmas**.

14th The Chinese conduct a nuclear test in Lop Nor which is a dried up lake.

15th West Gate Bridge, Australia .Two years into construction of the bridge, at 11:50 am on 15 October 1970, the 112 metres (367 ft) **span** between **piers** 10 and 11 collapsed and fell 50 metres (160 ft) to the ground and water below. Thirty-five construction workers were killed and 18 injured, making it Australia's worst industrial accident.

20th The announced objectives of Zond 8 were investigations of the Moon and circumlunar space and testing of onboard systems and units. The spacecraft obtained photographs of Earth on 21 October from a distance of 64,480 km. The spacecraft transmitted flight images of Earth for three days. Zond 8 flew past the Moon on October 24, 1970, at a distance of 1110.4 km and obtained both **black-and-white** and color photographs of the lunar surface

25th The wreck of the Confederate submarine Hunley is found off **Charleston, South Carolina**, by pioneer **underwater archaeologist**, Dr. E. Lee Spence, then just 22 years old. Hunley was the first submarine in history to sink a ship in warfare.

28th Gary Gabelich drives the rocket-powered Blue Flame to an official land speed record at 622.407 mph on the dry lake bed of the Bonneville Salt Flats in Utah. The record, the first above 1,000 km/h, stands for nearly 13 years.

November

1st Three Pakistanis and a Polish Deputy Foreign Minister, Zygfryd Wolniak, are killed at Karachi airport, Pakistan.

8th Tom Dempsey, who was born with a deformed right foot and right hand, sets a National Football League record by kicking a 63-yard field goal to lift the New Orleans Saints to a 19–17 victory over the Detroit Lions at Tulane Stadium.

13th **Bhola cyclone**: A 120-mph **tropical cyclone** hits the densely populated **Ganges Delta** region of **East Pakistan** (now **Bangladesh**), killing an estimated 500,000 people (considered the **20th century**'s worst cyclone disaster).

14th Southern Airways Flight 932 crashes in Wayne County, West Virginia; all 75 on board, including 37 players and 5 coaches from the Marshall University football team, are killed

20th The **Miss World 1970** beauty pageant, hosted by **Bob Hope** at the **Royal Albert Hall**, London is disrupted by Women's Liberation protesters. Earlier on the same evening a bomb is placed under a **BBC** outside broadcast vehicle by **The Angry Brigade**, in protest at the entry of separate black and white contestants by **South Africa**. **Jennifer Hosten** from Grenada won the crown of Miss World 1970.

23rd Rodgers and Hammerstein's Oklahoma! makes its network TV debut, when CBS telecasts the 1955 film version as a three-hour Thanksgiving special.

25th In Tokyo, author and **Tatenokai** militia leader **Yukio Mishima** and his followers take over the headquarters of the **Japan Self-Defence Forces** in an attempted **coup d'état**. After Mishima's speech fails to sway public opinion towards his right-wing political beliefs, including restoration of the powers of the **Emperor**. He later commits suicide.

27th Bolivian artist Benjamin Mendoza tries to assassinate **Pope Paul VI** during his visit in **Manila**.

28th The **Montréal Alouettes** defeated the **Calgary Stampeders** to become victors in the **58th Grey Cup** 23–10.

30th British Caledonian Airways Ltd. (BCal) is formed.

December

3rd In **Montreal**, kidnapped British Trade Commissioner **James Cross** is released by the **Front de libération du Québec** terrorist group after being held hostage for 60 days. Police negotiate his release and in return the Government of Canada grants 5 terrorists from the FLQ's Chenier Cell their request for safe passage to **Cuba**.

4th The U.N. announces that Portuguese navy and army units were responsible for the attempted invasion of Guinea.

7th During his visit to the Polish capital, **German Chancellor Willy Brandt** goes down on his knees in front of a monument to the victims of the **Warsaw Ghetto**, which will become known as the **Warschauer Kniefall** ("Warsaw Genuflection")

13th The government of Poland announces food price increases. Riots and looting lead to a bloody confrontation between the rioters and the government on **December 15**.

15th The USSR's Venera 7 becomes the first spacecraft to land successfully on Venus and transmit data back to Earth

17th The Ethiopian government declares a **state of emergency** in the county of Eritrea over the activities of the **Eritrean Liberation Front**.

21st United States build The **Grumman F-14 Tomcat** and makes its first flight.

23rd The Polish government freezes food prices for two years.

The North Tower of the World Trade Centre in New York City is topped out at 1,368 feet (417 m), making it the tallest building in the world.

28th In **Viscaya** in the **Basque country** of Spain, 15,000 go on strike in protest at the Burgos trial death sentences. **Francisco Franco** commutes the sentences to 30 years in prison.

30th Paul McCartney sues in Britain to dissolve **The Beatles'** legal partnership.

PEOPLE IN POWER

Queen Elizabeth was born in **London** as the first child of the Duke and Duchess of York, later **King George VI** and **Queen Elizabeth**, and she was educated privately at home. Her father acceded to the throne on the **abdication** of his brother **King Edward VIII** in 1936, from which time she was the **heir presumptive**. She began to undertake public duties **during the Second World War**, serving in the **Auxiliary Territorial Service**. In 1947, she married **Prince Philip, Duke of Edinburgh**, a former prince of Greece and Denmark, with whom she has four children: **Charles, Prince of Wales**; **Anne, Princess Royal**; **Prince Andrew, Duke of York**; and **Prince Edward, Earl of Wessex**.

Prince Charles

Princess Anne

Prince Andrew

Prince Edward

A year of elections

Harold Wilson
Prime Minister 1964-1970
and again in 1974-1976
Labour Party

Edward Heath
Prime Minster 1970-1974
Conservative Party

World leaders

Richard Nixon
U.S. President
1969-1974

Willy Brandt
Chancellor of Germany
1969-1974

Georges Pompidou
French President
1969-1974

John Gorton
Australia Prime Minister
1968-1971

The Year You Were Born 1970
Book by Sapphire Publishing
All rights reserved

Made in the USA
San Bernardino, CA
13 May 2019